D1061370

RECORD-BREAKING
AIRPLANES

DON BERLINER

 Lerner Publications Company • Minneapolis, Minnesota

ACKNOWLEDGMENTS: The photographs are reproduced through the courtesy of: pp. 6, 18, 38, 45, 55, 56, U.S. Air Force; pp. 7, 13, 14, 20, 34, Don Berliner; pp. 8, 9, 11, 12, 19 (top), 25, Smithsonian Institution; pp. 16, 19 (bottom), Musée de l'Air; pp. 17, 24, 27, 28, 29, Truman C. Weaver Collection; pp. 22, 44 (top), Vickers; p. 23, M.P. Marsh; pp. 30, 31, 33, Messerschmitt Archiv; p. 32, Hans Dieterle; p. 36 (top), Harry Gann (by Dusty Carter); pp. 36 (bottom), 37, Al Chute; p. 39, RAF Museum; pp. 40, 50, Lockheed Aircraft Company; pp. 41, 46 (top), 48 (bottom), 53 (top), McDonnell Douglas Corporation; pp. 42, 43, 46 (bottom), 48 (top), Rockwell International Corporation; p. 44 (bottom), Hawker Siddeley Aviation; p. 49, Flight International; p. 52, General Dynamics Corporation; p. 53 (bottom), Jay Miller; p. 54, National Aeronautics and Space Administration.

LIBRARY OF CONGRESS CATALOGING IN PUBLICATION DATA

Berliner, Don
    Record-Breaking Airplanes.

    (Superwheels & thrill sports)
    Summary: Traces the history of air-speed records from Santos Dumont's first official record in 1906 to the records broken by modern-day, supersonic aircraft.
    I. Airplanes—Speed records—Juvenile literature. [1. Airplanes—Speed records] I. Title. II. Series.
    TL711.A5B47 1985   629.13'09   84-15411
    ISBN 0-8225-0429-4 (lib. bdg.)

Copyright © 1985 by Lerner Publications Company

All rights reserved. International copyright secured. No part of this book may be reproduced in any form whatsoever without permission in writing from the publisher except for the inclusion of brief quotations in an acknowledged review.

Manufactured in the United States of America

International Standard Book Number: 0-8225-0429-4
Library of Congress Catalog Card Number: 84-15411

2 3 4 5 6 7 8 9 10 94 93 92 91 90 89 88 87 86 85

CONTENTS

THE SPEED CHALLENGE

To many, nothing is more thrilling than speeding through the sky in an airplane, pushing it to its limit and traveling faster than anyone before. It was soon after the Wright brothers' first airplane flight in 1903 that people wanted to know how fast planes could really fly. Less than three years later, the first official air speed record (ASR) was set, and the first airplane race was held in 1909.

If an air speed record is to be official, the timing and measuring must be done by the Fédération Aéronautique Internationale (FAI), the organization in charge of contests and official records for all types of air and space-craft. About 50 countries belong to the FAI, and the National Aeronautic Association (NAA) handles the FAI's work in the United States.

In the early days of aviation, an ASR could be set over a course of any length. But in 1920, the FAI decided that pilots should make their speed runs around a four-kilometer square course (one kilometer, or .6 mile, on each side) so their speed wouldn't be affected by how hard the wind was blowing. Later that same year, the FAI ruled that two straight runs must be made with the wind and two against it, with the final speed determined by averaging the times of the four runs.

As airplanes traveled faster, it became harder to time them for such short runs. So in 1923, the course was lengthened to three kilometers (1.86 miles). To set a record, a pilot could fly no higher than 100 meters (328 feet) above the ground. Then in the 1950s, the FAI changed its rules and allowed jet-propelled airplanes to fly at higher altitudes and be tracked and timed by radar because it was too dangerous for them to fly so close to the ground at such high speeds.

Timed by ultra-sensitive electronic equipment, Frank Everest thunders to a new world speed record (see page 45).

The current ASR, set in 1979, was made by an airplane flying at 80,000 feet, or more than 15 miles above the ground. When the first ASR was set in 1906, it is unlikely that anyone ever imagined how fast airplanes would fly 70 years later.

Today the 1903 Wright *Flyer* is on display in Washington's National Air and Space Museum.

THE EARLY BIRDS

The first successful manned airplane flight was made on December 17, 1903. Watched by his brother, Wilbur, Orville Wright struggled through the air for 12 seconds in his Wright *Flyer* for a distance of 120 feet before landing on the sands of Kitty Hawk, North Carolina. His wasn't an official speed record, however. No one thought about speed then, and there wasn't anyone to check his flight to make it official. What was important was simply that Wright had flown. Speed and altitude really didn't matter.

Santos-Dumont set the first official world air speed record in this frail-looking aircraft.

The first official ASR was set by Alberto Santos-Dumont, a 95-pound airplane designer/builder from Brazil. Well known for flying small *dirigibles* (powered airships) around Paris, Santos-Dumont set the ASR in France in 1906. The FAI hadn't been organized yet, so the Aéro Club of France provided timers to clock speed runs by anyone wanting to try for a French record. Santos-Dumont's *biplane* (a plane with double wings on each side of its body) had its propellor at the rear and the tail in the front. Alberto stood up while flying, perhaps so he could get out quickly if it looked like the airplane might crash! Santos-Dumont's first ASR was only 25.6 miles per hour (mph). At that time, the

Glenn Curtiss (in necktie) flew this biplane to an ASR in 1909.

Wright brothers were already flying at 40 mph, but they were more interested in improving their airplanes than in setting records.

By 1909, when the first air race was held at Reims, France, the ASR had only increased to 34 mph. The contestants at Reims were ready to raise the record much higher, and tens of thousands watched for a full week as more than 20 pilots battled strong winds and heavy rain. For the very first time, airplanes raced together around a race course, and almost every race brought a new ASR.

At the Reims race, James Gordon Bennett, a world-famous newspaper owner who wanted to encourage people to build better and faster airplanes, presented the first major air racing trophy. The Gordon Bennett Trophy was given to Glenn Curtiss, who became the first American to set an ASR when he flew his biplane at 43.4 mph.

Curtiss, the first important American aviator since the Wright brothers, had begun his aviation career by working closely with Alexander Graham Bell, who was then an airplane designer. Curtiss had built several airplanes, and he later built America's first seaplane.

The record that Curtiss set at Reims was not to last for long, however. Before the meet was over, the ASR was held by Louis Blériot, who flew 47.8 mph in his *monoplane* (a plane with single wings on each side of the body). Blériot's monoplane could travel faster with less power than a biplane because its single wing created less wind resistance, or *drag*. It wasn't as easy to build monoplanes as strong as biplanes, however. Biplanes were stronger because many more wires and braces could be built between the wings. At the time, people weren't ready to give up strength for speed, so biplanes remained more popular than monoplanes. The next air speed records, however, would be set with monoplanes.

The first big leap forward in the ASR came in 1910 when pilots began to put bigger engines in their Blériot monoplanes. These planes all had *rotary* engines. While rotary engines were light and powerful, the airplanes were difficult to fly because the engine revolved as fast as the propellor.

Edward Nieuport built the first airplane in which *streamlining* made a difference in the plane's performance, and, in 1911, he broke the ASR three times. Nieuport's airplanes were light with small engines, and most of their parts were tucked away inside. Even the engine in the nose was partly covered by a metal cowling. People were now beginning to learn that in designing planes for speed, streamlining was more important than horsepower (h.p.).

In 1912, Deperdussin, a new French company, began building small, streamlined

In the same Reims air race, Louis Blériot broke Curtiss' record by 4.4 mph. Unfortunately, Blériot wrecked his monoplane on the final day of the meet.

monoplanes that soon were being used for speed-record flying. The fuselage of the "Dep" was completely enclosed, and there was an aluminum cowling around the engine. A rounded skid stuck out from under the plane in front to protect the propellor if the airplane tipped up on its nose.

Late that year during the Gordon Bennett Trophy Race on a four-mile course near Chicago, Illinois, a "Dep" with a 140-h.p.

This 1912 Deperdussin monoplane was the first airplane to fly faster than 100 miles per hour.

engine boosted the ASR to 108 mph. The airplane was flown by Jules Vedrines, who earlier that year had officially become the first person to fly faster than 100 mph.

The Deperdussin factory brought out a much more streamlined racer in 1913. That plane had a bullet-shaped cowling around its 140-h.p. rotary engine and a large spinner around the hub of the propellor. It had a small windshield to protect the pilot from the wind blast and a long headrest that tapered back to the tail. The landing gear was streamlined to reduce wind resistance as much as possible.

This 1913 "Dep," the first truly streamlined speed-record airplane, was piloted by Maurice Prevost. He increased the ASR to 112 mph and then, with a new 160-h.p. engine, flew the same airplane at 127 mph. (That was 15 miles per hour *slower* than the land speed record held by "Wild Bob" Burman in a Benz racing car!)

All of the speed records set during the first years of flying were made by civilian pilots in civilian airplanes because not many military planes had been built yet. But when World War I started in 1914, many planes were built for military use.

This restored 1913 Deperdussin can be seen at the Musée de l'Air in Paris.

The Nieuport-Delage was one of the World War I biplanes that was streamlined for post-war ASR attempts. This model hangs in the Musée de l'Air.

FASTER AND BETTER BIPLANES

World War I put a stop to record breaking, but not to the production of airplanes. Most of the thousands of airplanes built during the war were biplanes because the pilots who flew them felt that only airplanes with two wings were strong enough. As a result, the progress with monoplanes was forgotten during the war years.

When the war ended in 1918, many left-over airplanes were sold for a few hundred dollars to anyone who wanted to get into the flying business. While these planes weren't very fast or very streamlined, they were cheap, and they were the planes that were flown when the FAI resumed record keeping in 1920. During the war, much had been learned about how to make airplanes fly faster, higher, and further, and many people started to set records for not only speed but also for distance and altitude.

Improved models of military pursuit and scouting planes set the first air speed records after the war. Most of these planes were built by such well-known French companies as SPAD and Nieuport, and their success kept the ASR in France, where it had been since 1909.

Partly because of the great rivalry that developed between two French pilots—Sadi Lecointe, who flew a Nieuport 29V, and Bernard de Romanet, who flew a SPAD 20—the speed-record race became very exciting. Lecointe and de Romanet took turns breaking each other's ASR; every time one of them would set a record, the other would come back to set a new one. In 1920, Lecointe became the first person to set a speed record after the war, and his 171 mph was a big increase over the old record of 127 mph that had been set in 1913.

Almost immediately, de Romanet raised the record to 182 mph, and then Lecointe came back with an ASR of 188 mph. De Romanet was determined to regain his lead and flew his SPAD 20 at 192 mph. His new ASR did not last long, however, as Lecointe then

Bernard de Romanet poses alongside his SPAD 20 biplane.

set three straight records, including one at 212 mph in 1922. Only 10 years after the 100-mph barrier had been broken, the first ASR of more than 200 mph was set.

It was not until 1922 that the United States began work on the first airplanes designed only for speed. That year, Billy Mitchell, a U.S. Army general, set the first ASR by an American since 1909. Mitchell's Curtiss R-6 army racer was the most streamlined in the world at that time. It had a very pointed nose, and every part was designed to slice through the air at the greatest possible speed. Flying on a course at Detroit, Michigan, Mitchell easily raised the speed record to 223 mph.

Both Billy Mitchell and Russell Maughan flew the Curtiss R-6 racer, the first airplane designed especially for breaking air speed records.

Flying at 233 mph in a Nieuport-Delage *sesquiplane* (a biplane with very small bottom wings), Sadi Lecointe came right back the following year to take the ASR away from the United States. Then another U.S. Army pilot, Russell Maughan, recaptured the ASR at 237 mph in a Curtiss R-6 racer. Such fierce competition between the United States and France was sure to produce better and faster airplanes.

Billy Mitchell

Later that year, a new U.S. Navy racer, the Curtiss R2C-1, appeared. It was the most streamlined biplane yet, with a screaming 500-h.p. engine. Harold Brow and Al Williams piloted this racer, and, when they finished their series of speed runs, they had raised the ASR to 267 mph. After that, the army and navy quit setting speed records for awhile because they were concerned about the danger of racing airplanes at such high speeds.

A year later, the French brought the ASR back "home" with the first speed-record monoplane, the Bernard V.2. Flying at 279 mph, Florentin Bonnett showed the world that a 600-h.p. monoplane was faster than any biplane. Now, 11 years after the last record had been set in a monoplane, monoplanes once again became the landplane record setters.

Between 1920 and 1924, the ASR had increased by more than 100 mph. Bonnett's 279-mph record seemed incredibly fast—even dangerous—to most people. But that speed would be commonplace in only a few years.

Above: Two Curtiss R2C-1 biplanes like those flown by Harold Brow and Al Williams. *Below:* Florentin Bonnett's Bernard V.2 monoplane, one of the first modern monoplanes.

A close-up of the Macchi MC.72 seaplane. The MC.72 holds the ASR for propellor-driven seaplanes (see page 24).

SPEEDY SEAPLANES

During the early years of aviation, the air speed records had been set by *landplanes,* planes with wheels for taking off and landing on grass runways. (There were no concrete runways yet.) Airplanes didn't have much room to accelerate to high speed for taking off because the runways were short, so they were designed with large wings for quick take-offs. But planes with large wings could not fly as fast as those with smaller wings.

One kind of aircraft, however, was built for "runways" made of water. These *seaplanes* had boat-shaped attachments or bottoms called *pontoons* instead of wheels. Even though their *pontoons* slowed them down, seaplanes could be built with smaller wings to fly faster than landplanes.

Many fast seaplanes had been built in the 1920s because a wealthy Frenchman, Jacques Schneider, offered a valuable trophy for a seaplane race. He thought the prize would encourage people to improve seaplanes, and he was right. While the first Schneider Trophy races had been held before World War I, really fast seaplanes were not built until the race became famous about 10 years later.

In 1927, Mario de Bernardi, flying an Italian Macchi M.52 racing seaplane in Venice, set an ASR for seaplanes and also broke the landplane record (photograph on page 25). His 298 mph ASR surprised many people, who thought that all seaplanes were slow. De Bernardi broke his own record the following year when he flew an improved Macchi M.52R to a new ASR of 319 mph. Meanwhile, the landplane record stayed at 279 mph.

A. H. Orlebar's S.6 was the first Supermarine seaplane to set an ASR.

A year later, the British were ready to fly their new racers. They were equipped with huge 1,900-h.p. engines, the most powerful yet in any kind of airplane. The Supermarine won the 1929 Schneider Trophy Race at 329 mph on a 31-mile race course. A few days later, A. H. Orlebar used the same seaplane to set an ASR of 358 mph.

The last Schneider Trophy Race was held in 1931, and again the British won easily. With their newest 2,350-h.p. Supermarine S.6B, John Boothman won the race at 340 mph. Flying the same plane just a few days later, George Stainforth became the first person to travel faster than 400 mph when he set an ASR of 407 mph on the morning of September 29, 1931.

The British had won the Schneider Race three times in a row, and they were allowed to keep the trophy after the final race. But

The Supermarine S.6B won the last Schneider Trophy Race and later became the first plane to travel faster than 400 miles per hour.

the Italians had been working on a new racing seaplane, and they wanted to set an ASR, even if there weren't any races to win. Their Macchi MC.72 was long and slim with two large pontoons underneath like the Supermarine racer. But there was one big difference. The MC.72 had two propellors in its nose, one behind the other, and the plane was driven

The ASR set by Francesco Agello in this Macchi MC.72 seaplane in 1934 still stands.

by two powerful engines.

Five MC.72 seaplanes were built, but two crashed on test flights. In 1933, Francesco Agello took off from a lake in northern Italy near the Alps in one of the remaining racers. He flew along a speed course at an average speed of 424 mph to set a new ASR. Then he flew an improved MC.72 to raise the ASR to 441 mph the following year.

After 50 years, the record set by Agello in the MC.72 is still the ASR for propellor-driven seaplanes. And since so few people are interested in racing seaplanes today, there is a good chance that it will still be the record 50 years from now. That record deserves to stand forever because it is the fastest that anyone has ever flown in an airplane with an open cockpit. With winds blowing past him at more than 400 mph, Agello had only a small windshield for protection.

Fuel is added to the Macchi M.52, the first seaplane to fly faster than any landplane.

During the 1920s and 1930s, governments had been willing to spend millions of dollars to support seaplane racing, and countries that built record-setting airplanes were recognized as leaders in aviation. There was no support for landplane racing, however, so pilots who wanted to break the landplane ASR had to do it without government funds.

PYLON RACERS

While air speed records were held by racing seaplanes from 1927 until 1939, some very fine landplanes were also being built. Some of the most exciting were the custom-built airplanes that were flown in closed-course pylon races like the Cleveland (Ohio) National Air Races. In pylon racing, airplanes fly around an aerial racetrack with tall, brightly colored towers, or *pylons,* at each corner so pilots will be able to stay on course and not cut inside on the turns, which would disqualify them from the race.

The airplanes flown in pylon races were built in small workshops and garages by amateur racers. Because the owners didn't receive any government funding, they couldn't afford to buy huge engines for their planes. Instead they built small, light airplanes that could fly fast without much horsepower.

Piloted by American Jimmy Doolittle, the most famous of these civilian raceplanes, the GeeBee Super Sportster, broke the landplane ASR that the French had held for eight years. The GeeBee was shaped like a barrel, but it was much more streamlined than it looked. The plane's fuselage tapered back from its broad nose to its tiny tail, and the nose contained an 800-h.p. radial engine. In order to balance the heavy engine up front, the pilot sat back near the tail where, unfortunately, he couldn't see very well.

The GeeBee was built purely for speed. With it, Doolittle won the 1932 Thompson Trophy Race at 252 mph and then set a straight-dash ASR at 294 mph. While the red-and-white "flying milk bottle" was a difficult airplane to fly because of its shape, it was a great racer.

Jimmy Doolittle's GeeBee Super Sportster

One year later, another famous racing pilot, Jimmy Wedell, flew his 1,000-h.p. Wedell-Williams racer even faster than the GeeBee. When he raised the landplane ASR to 305 mph, he became the first civilian pilot to fly faster than 300 mph. Unfortunately, both of these airplanes were wrecked in racing accidents not long after they had set records.

The French were not happy that the Americans had taken the landplane ASR away from them, and they wanted it back. To challenge the record, the French prepared one of their great Caudron racers. Smaller and lighter than either of the American racers, it had an engine of only 340 h.p. Because of its streamlining, it didn't need as much

In 1933 Jimmy Wedell's home-built racer flew faster than any military plane.

power, and Raymond Delmotte was able to fly at a speed of 314 mph and bring the ASR back to France in 1934.

By now, another famous American pilot, Howard Hughes, had become interested in speed racing and was determined to set an ASR. Hughes, well known as a movie producer as well as a pilot, hired a group of engineers to build an ASR airplane that he had designed. Hughes' was one of the first high-speed planes to be built primarily from aluminum, and it was the most streamlined in the world at the time. It was the first plane to have all of the rivet heads filed off even with the aluminum skin so they wouldn't stick out to cause more wind resistance and slow down the airplane.

Above: In 1935, Howard Hughes set an ASR in an airplane that he had designed, the most streamlined in the world at the time. *Below:* The Caudron C.460 racer. Following Raymond Delmotte's 1934 ASR, Michel Detroyat won pylon races with the plane in Los Angeles in 1936.

All of Hughes' advanced ideas worked. He packed a 1,000-h.p. engine into the small cowling of his H-1 and was able to set an ASR for landplanes at 352 mph in 1935. While Hughes' record was almost 100 mph slower than the seaplane ASR of 441 mph, the technical advances in landplane design would soon make them the speed leaders in the sky.

Willy Messerschmitt, designer of the Me-209, congratulates pilot Fritz Wendel on setting an ASR in 1939 (see page 33).

NAZI PROPAGANDA

Politics was involved in the next series of attempts on the landplane air speed record. In Germany, Hitler's Nazis were laying the groundwork for what would be World War II. One of their tactics was to frighten other countries into believing that Germany was mightier than any other nation in the world, and part of their plan was to show that their airplanes were superior to anyone else's. Using special speed-record airplanes but telling the world they were flying regular military planes, the Nazis decided to go after the ASR. As a result, Germany hoped that other countries would think they would not stand a chance against the fast German planes in air battles.

In 1937, a factory-built Messerschmitt Bf-109 was modified for an attempt at the ASR. Its

The Messerschmitt Bf-109 was a modified racer and not a standard-model fighter, as the public had been told.

cockpit was lowered and streamlined, and the regular engine was replaced by a more powerful racing engine. With this special airplane, Hermann Wurster, chief test pilot for Messerschmitt, set a landplane ASR of 380 mph. But after his flight, the Nazis released photographs showing a regular fighter-plane, not a racer. The world was fooled, and it looked like Germany had the fastest fighter-planes on earth.

Now two of Germany's biggest airplane companies, Messerschmitt and Heinkel, started building special ASR planes, and, in 1939, both companies had airplanes ready to try to break the 441-mph ASR set by Francesco Agello five years earlier. Since very few people had seen these special speed-record planes, their secret could be kept.

In April 1939, Hans Dieterle flew the Heinkel He-100 to a new ASR of 464 mph. The public,

This plane was *not* the Heinkel He-113, as first reported, but a superbly streamlined He-100.

however, was told that he had set the record in a regular production-line He-113, an airplane that had never been built! The He-100 was so hard to fly that, said Dieterle, it was like "handling a raw egg." Aviation people outside of Germany didn't know about the nonexistent He-113 and thought they would have to fight these super-fast planes if a war started.

A few weeks later, the Messerschmitt ASR plane was wheeled out. Called the Me-109R, it was described as a racing version of the standard fighterplane. Instead, it was really

The Messerschmitt Me-209 that was flown by Fritz Wendel. The Me-209 held the ASR for piston-engine airplanes from 1939 to 1969.

a research plane, the Me-209. Fritz Wendel flew the Me-209 to break the ASR with a flight clocked at 469 mph. The only photographs of the airplane showed so little that no one knew they had been fooled.

All during World War II, pilots looked for these "mystery" airplanes. But, of course, no one ever saw them because they didn't exist! The special airplanes that had set the ASRs were so hard to fly that only the best test pilots could be trusted with them. It wasn't until after the war that people learned they had been tricked into thinking that Germany had such fast military airplanes.

In 1969, Darryl Greenamyer's Grumman Bearcat finally broke the German ASR for piston-engine airplanes.

MODERN CIVILIAN PLANES

In the years following World War II, the jet airplane became the center of attention in the air speed race, and people paid less and less attention to propellor-driven airplanes. Since 1939, the German Messerschmitt Me-209 had held the air speed record for propellor-driven airplanes, and it wasn't until the late 1960s that racing pilots became interested in breaking that record. Several considered fixing up their *Unlimited Class racers* (airplanes with piston engines of any size) for a try at the ASR for *props* (propellor-driven airplanes), but only one man put his ideas into action.

Darryl Greenamyer knew a lot about speed flying because he was a test pilot for Lockheed, a builder of jet planes. He had won the important race at the National Championships in Reno, Nevada, several times and flew a gleaming white Grumman Bearcat. After several failures because of mechanical problems, Greenamyer again tried to break the ASR for props in 1969. His 3,000-h.p. Bearcat was lighter and more streamlined than any other Unlimited Class racer in history. Flying no higher than 100 feet above the ground, Greenamyer made four passes over the three-kilometer course at Edwards Air Force Base in California at an average speed of 482 mph. That speed was fast enough to take the 30-year ASR away from the Germans.

In 1977, Darryl Greenamyer was back. This time, he flew a "home-built" F-104 Starfighter that had been constructed over a 10-year period from parts and pieces bought one at a time. Because the plane didn't have any heavy guns or armor plating to protect the pilot from enemy attack, it was a lot lighter than the F-104s used by the U.S. Air Force.

Above: Darryl Greenamyer's home-built F-104 Starfighter. *Below:* Steve Hinton's Red Baron RB-51.

Hinton's Red Baron in the air. In 1979, Hinton broke Greenamyer's ASR for piston engines.

Darryl flew this unusual plane to a new ASR of 997 mph, but he failed to set a record for altitude. Before he could exceed the 123,500-foot record that had been set by an experimental Soviet airplane earlier in the year, Greenamyer had to bail out of his plane when one of its wheels refused to come down for a landing.

In 1979, Greenamyer's prop-driven ASR was broken by another Unlimited Class racer, the Red Baron RB-51, flown by Steve Hinton. Hinton's modified P-51 Mustang had a large Rolls-Royce Griffon 3,000-h.p. engine and two propellors like the 1934 Macchi MC.72 seaplane. Steve flew the plane at 499 mph for a new record but wrecked it soon afterwards during the Reno Air Races.

Colonel Al Boyd buckles on his parachute before attempting an ASR in 1947 (see page 40).

THE FIRST JET AIRPLANES

During World War II, many new developments had been made in the design of airplanes, and hundreds of thousands of planes had been built. While many of them had flown faster than the current air speed record, their speeds were unofficial because the FAI had kept no records during the war.

The jet engine was the most important new idea in airplane construction to come out of the war. Until a jet was tested in Germany in 1939, all airplanes had used propellors. Even the first jets were faster than any propellor planes, and, by the time the war was over, a number of jet planes had reached speeds in excess of 500 mph.

Although the Germans may have had the fastest jets during the war, the peace treaty they had signed at the end of the war prohibited them from building or flying any planes. This gave the British the lead in jet develop-

The British Gloster Meteor fighter was the first jet plane to hold the world air speed record.

ment, but the United States was close behind.

It took a while for the FAI to start keeping air records again because the Germans had occupied their headquarters in Paris during the war. But in 1946, they were ready to see just how much faster the new jet planes really were. The British, eager to prove their planes the fastest, readied their sleek Gloster Meteor twin-engine fighter for a try at the ASR by removing its guns and giving it a smooth new paint job.

Pilot Hugh Wilson's speed over a three-kilometer course averaged 606 mph, making him the first person to fly faster than 500 mph. Then, flying another Meteor, Edward Donaldson increased the ASR to 616 mph the following year. For the first time in 15 years, the British were the world speed champions, and there was no question about how fast their new jets were.

Al Boyd's "Racey" being refueled at Edwards Air Force Base, California

Next, it was the United States's turn. Their first jet, the Bell Airacomet, was a big disappointment and turned out to be no faster than a propellor plane. But soon the faster Lockheed P-80 Shooting Star came along, a plane that was a pleasure to fly. In a modified P-80 that had bigger air intakes, a super-slick paint job, and was nicknamed "Racey," Al Boyd flew 624 mph to bring the ASR back to the United States in 1947 for the first time since 1923.

It didn't make the navy or the marines very happy when Boyd, a U.S. Army Air Force officer, was called the world's fastest pilot.

Two ASRs were set by the U.S. Navy's Douglas Skystreak in 1947.

Soon a rivalry developed among the U.S. military branches, and each wanted to have the fastest pilot. To achieve this goal, the U.S. Navy created the Douglas D-558-I, a special research jet. Named the Skystreak, it was fast enough to set two more ASRs in 1947. First, U.S. Navy pilot Turner Caldwell boosted the ASR to 641 mph. Then marine pilot Marion Carl pushed the Skystreak up to 651 mph. The British didn't have any airplanes that could challenge such incredible speeds, so the race was an all-American one for several years.

Determined to become the U.S. leader once again, the air force took the record away from the marines in one of its first new F-86

The U.S. Army Air Force Sabrejet

Sabrejets with swept-back wings. Richard Johnson flew the Sabrejet at 671 mph to set the fourth ASR that year, a record that would not be broken for five years.

In 1952, the U.S. Air Force challenged its own record. Its improved Sabrejet had the extra power of an *afterburner*, a device in the jet's tailpipe that added fuel to ignite the hot blast of exhaust. This caused a long flame to come out the back of the jet, making the plane even noisier than a regular jet. Flying the new F-86D Sabre at Salton Sea in southern California, J. Slade Nash set an ASR at 699 mph. And the following year, William Barns increased the ASR to 716 mph in a similar plane. There was now no doubt that the Sabre

William Barns flew an improved Sabrejet to a new 716-mph ASR in 1953.

was the finest jet fighter in the world.

During 1953, the ASR changed five times. After Barns set his 716-mph record, the British were ready to get back into the race. Flying a beautiful bright red Hawker Hunter fighter at 728 mph, Neville Duke took the record away from the United States. A few days later, Mike Lithgow, another Englishman, flew one of the first Supermarine Swift fighters at 736 mph for still another new ASR.

Mike Lithgow's Supermarine Swift *(above)* broke the ASR that had been set by Neville Duke's Hawker Hunter *(below)*.

At almost the same time, the U.S. Navy was trying out its newest delta-winged F4D Skyray fighter. This airplane had very wide wings and no horizontal tail. Fast and very maneuverable, it was copied by many other airplane designers. James Verdin flew the Skyray at 753 mph for the fourth ASR of that record-breaking year.

The final ASR of 1953 was set in October when the U.S. Air Force tried out its brand new F-100 Super Sabre. In the Sabre, Frank Everest set a record of 755 mph, the last *subsonic* (less than the speed of sound) ASR. At that time, people thought it would be very difficult to control an airplane flying at the speed of sound: 760 mph at sea level. But little by little, ASR speeds were creeping up toward *Mach 1* (the speed of sound). It would be the Super Sabre that would break through the sound barrier.

U.S. Air Force captain J. Slade Nash set a 1952 ASR in this Sabrejet (see page 42).

Above: James Verdin set the fourth ASR of 1953 in this U.S. Navy Skyray. *Below:* Later that year, the last subsonic ASR was set by a U.S. Air Force Super Sabre.

SUPERSONIC FLIGHT

Flying an improved version of the Super Sabre, Harold Hanes set the first supersonic air speed record in August 1955. Since it was dangerous to fly so fast at a low altitude, the FAI established some new rules. Pilots could now set an ASR while flying at any altitude because, even though a plane might be flying several miles high, it could still be timed very accurately with radar. Hane's exciting flight of 822 mph over the Mojave Desert had brought speed records into the supersonic age.

The following year, the British surprised everyone by completely smashing the ASR. Peter Twiss flew a Fairey Delta II research jet at an amazing 1,132 mph to add more than 300 mph to the ASR. The Fairey Delta II had a nose that could be lowered so the pilot could see over it better during take-offs and landings. (This idea worked so well that it was later used on the Concorde supersonic airliner.) While the last planes to set ASRs had been combat planes modified for record attempts, the Delta II had been built strictly for high-speed flying.

During the next few years, the U.S. government did not want any of its terrific new jet fighters used for speed records because they didn't want other countries to know just how fast the fighters were. But in 1957, Adrian Drew was finally allowed to fly a McDonnell F-101 Voodoo twin-engine jet for an ASR attempt. Thanks to a pair of jet engines, each producing 15,000 pounds of thrust, Drew was clocked at 1,208 mph. Since all airplanes were now very streamlined, more and more power was necessary for increased speed.

Above: In 1955, Harold Hanes flew this Super Sabre to the first supersonic ASR. *Below:* Adrian Drew set an ASR in the Voodoo jet in 1957.

Peter Twiss flew the Fairey Delta II at 1,132 mph in 1956 to return the ASR to Great Britain.

The F-104 Starfighter was flown to an ASR by Walter Irwin in 1958.

An even newer U.S. Air Force jet was allowed to try for the ASR in 1958. Called "the missile with a man in it," the Lockheed F-104 Starfighter had a long fuselage and stubby little wings. Walter Irwin set an ASR of 1,404 mph with the F-104. That was more than twice the speed of sound (at that altitude) and much faster than any British jet could fly.

The next year, the aviation world got a big surprise. The next pilot to set an ASR was a Russian, Georgi Mossolov, who flew a mysterious airplane, the E-66, at 1,484 mph. No one knew anything about this first Soviet airplane to set an ASR, not even what it looked like. But several years later, experts decided that it probably resembled the MiG-21, a jet fighter that was built in the Soviet Union and used by most eastern European countries.

Only a few weeks after the U.S.S.R. had proved they had the fastest airplanes in the world, the United States answered back. Now it was more important to top the Soviet record than to keep secret the performance of a new fighter. U.S. Air Force Colonel Joseph Rogers climbed into a powerful Convair F-106 Delta Dart and flew to an ASR of 1,526 (about Mach 2.3). The Dart's engine developed almost 26,000 pounds of thrust, which, at that speed, was equal to about 60,000 h.p.

For two years, there were no attempts on the ASR. Then the U.S. Navy's hottest jet, the McDonnell F4H Phantom II, had its chance for fame. The Phantom II, the first navy fighter to be used by the air force, was also bought by other countries, and many were used in Vietnam. In 1961, U.S. Marine Corps pilot "Robbie" Robinson flew one of the early Phantom IIs at 1,606 mph for a new ASR. His plane was not a machine built for making speed records, however. Basically, it was the same airplane that military pilots were flying every day.

The following year, the Soviet air force got back into the ASR race with a second mystery plane. Colonel Mossolov, flying an E-166, broke the Phantom's record with a speed of 1,666 mph. Once again, the Soviets didn't reveal much about the airplane at the time. Later, however, the plane was put on display in a museum near Moscow. Then everyone could see that it was a special scientific research plane and not a standard production model.

Since FAI rules allowed the country trying for a record to provide all of the officials at the speed attempt, only the Russians knew much about the E-166's flight. But when people finally got a close look at the plane, they could see it was capable of flying at least as fast as the Soviets had claimed.

In 1959, Joseph Ropers set an ASR at 1,526 mph in the Delta Dart.

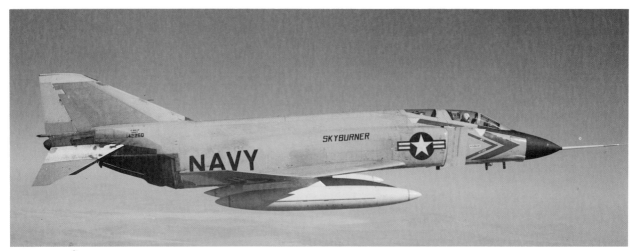

Above: The Phantom II, a production-model U.S. Navy jet, set an ASR in 1961. *Below:* Several years after setting an ASR of 1,666 mph, the mysterious Soviet E-166 was finally shown to the public.

The U.S. Air Force YF-12A Blackbird set a 2,070-mph ASR in 1965.

Now the U.S. military became concerned. They did not want the world to think that Soviet airplanes were better than American models. So to prove that U.S. planes were the best, the fastest U.S. jet, the YF-12A Blackbird, was unveiled in 1965. The Blackbird, a spy plane designed to fly very fast at very high altitudes, had been kept secret for a long time.

The Blackbird was one of the strangest-looking airplanes in the world. Totally black in color, its huge engines, which used a special high-altitude fuel, were tucked in close to its long, flat fuselage, and its delta-shaped wings were short. It had a tiny cockpit near the nose, and the two large vertical tails at the rear of the plane slanted in toward each other.

At Edwards Air Force Base, Colonel Robert Stephens' record runs were made at an altitude of 80,000 feet—more than 15 miles—so the plane could not be seen from the ground. But the radar equipment at the base could follow the plane very accurately as it sped along at better than 2,000 mph. Stephens' official ASR averaged 2,070 mph, or more than *three times* the speed of sound. (At that speed, Stephens could have flown from Los Angeles to New York in little more than an hour!)

If the Soviets had an airplane that could fly faster than the Blackbird, they weren't about to let anyone know. Stephens' ASR remained the official world's best for more than 10 years, and then it was beaten by another model of the same plane.

Even though it looked like no other country was going to challenge it, the U.S. Air Force decided to break its own record in 1976. That year, a new version of the YF-12, the SR-71, made a series of speed runs and broke a whole collection of records. Several different two-man crews were used for the record flights, and Eldon Joersz, who flew higher than 80,000 feet, set an ASR of 2,194 mph.

The Blackbird's crew, including pilot Robert Stephens *(left)*, after their record flight

The improved SR-71 Blackbird has held the ASR since 1976. Many believe it can fly at least 300 miles faster than its 2,194-mph ASR.

Blackbirds have held the ASR since 1965, and they may keep the record for a long time. Even if the United States or another country were to build a faster airplane, it may not want to let the rest of the world in on its secrets. And because the cost of setting an ASR in a fast jet plane is so great, only the most prosperous countries can even think about trying. Future speed-record attempts, therefore, will be made by individuals in special classes rather than by jet planes. Pilots will be trying for records for light planes in all different weight classes and types of engines—piston, turboprop, and turbojet—and for records in seaplanes, amphibians, gliders, and helicopters. They will be making runs over courses that are as short as 3 and as long as 5,000 kilometers. But no matter which record a pilot is trying to break, the attempt will be just as exciting as it was when Santos-Dumont set the first ASR of 25.6 mph in 1906.

THE WORLD'S AIR SPEED RECORDS

YEAR	PILOT	AIRPLANE	COURSE	SPEED (mph)
1906	Alberto Santos-Dumont	Santos-Dumont	Bagatelle,France	25.6
1907	Henri Farman	Farman	Issy, France	32.7
1909	Paul Tissandier	Wright	Pau, France	34.1
1909	Glenn Curtiss	Curtiss Reims	Reims, France	43.4
1909	Louis Blériot	Blériot	Reims, France	47.8
1910	Hubert Latham	Antoinette	Nice, France	48.2
1910	Leon Morane	Blériot	Reims, France	65.3
1910	Alfred Leblanc	Blériot	Blemont Park, New York	67.8
1911	Alfred Leblanc	Blériot	Pau, France	69.5
1911	Edward Nieuport	Nieuport	Chalons, France	74.4
1911	Alfred Leblanc	Blériot	Etampes, France	77.7
1911	Edward Nieuport	Nieuport	Chalons, France	80.8
1911	Edward Nieuport	Nieuport	Chalons, France	82.7
1912	Jules Vedrines	Deperdussin	Pau, France	90.2
1912	Jules Vedrines	Deperdussin	Pau, France	100.2
1912	Jules Vedrines	Deperdussin	Pau, France	100.9
1912	Jules Vedrines	Deperdussin	Pau, France	103.7
1912	Jules Vedrines	Deperdussin	Pau, France	104.3
1912	Jules Vedrines	Deperdussin	Reims, France	106.1
1912	Jules Vedrines	Deperdussin	Chicago, Illinois	108.2
1913	Maurice Prevost	Deperdussin	Reims, France	111.7
1913	Maurice Prevost	Deperdussin	Reims, France	119.2
1913	Maurice Prevost	Deperdussin	Reims, France	126.7
1920	Sadi Lecointe	Nieuport 29V	Villacoublay, France	171.0
1920	Jean Casale	SPAD 20bis[4]	Villacoublay, France	176.1
1920	Bernard de Romanet	SPAD 20bis[6]	Buc, France	181.9
1920	Sadi Lecointe	Nieuport 29V	Buc, France	184.4
1920	Sadi Lecointe	Nieuport 29V	Villacoublay, France	188.0
1920	Bernard de Romanet	SPAD 20bis[6]	Villacoublay, France	192.0
1920	Sadi Lecointe	Nieuport 29Vbis	Villacoublay, France	194.5
1921	Sadi Lecointe	Nieuport-Delage	Villesauvage, France	205.2
1922	Sadi Lecointe	Nieuport-Delage	Villesauvage, France	211.9
1922	William Mitchell	Curtiss R-6	Detroit, Michigan	223.0
1923	Sadi Lecointe	Nieuport-Delage	Istres, France	233.0
1923	Russell Maughan	Curtiss R-6	Dayton, Ohio	236.6
1923	Harold Brow	Curtiss R2C-1	Mineola, New York	259.1
1923	Al Williams	Curtiss R2C-1	Mineola, New York	266.6
1924	Florentin Bonnett	Bernard V.2	Istres, France	278.5
1927	Mario de Bernardi	Macchi M.52	Venice, Italy	297.8

1928	Mario de Bernardi	Macchi M.52R	Venice, Italy	318.6
1929	A. H. Orlebar	Supermarine S.6	Calshot, England	357.7
1931	George Stainforth	Supermarine S.6B	Lee-on-Solent, England	407.0
1932	Jimmy Doolittle	GeeBee R-1	Cleveland, Ohio	294.4[1]
1933	Francesco Agello	Macchi MC.72	Lake Garda, Italy	423.8
1933	Jimmy Wedell	Wedell-Williams	Glenview, Illinois	304.5[1]
1934	Francesco Agello	Macchi MC.72	Lake Garda, Italy	440.7
1934	Raymond Delmotte	Caudron C.460	Istres, France	314.3[1]
1935	Howard Hughes	Hughes H-1	Santa Ana, California	352.4[1]
1937	Hermann Wurster	Messerschmitt Bf-109E	Augsburg, Germany	379.6[1]
1939	Hans Dieterle	Heinkel He-100V	Oranienburg, Germany	463.9
1939	Fritz Wendel	Messerschmitt Me-209V	Augsburg, Germany	469.2
1945	Hugh Wilson	Gloster Meteor IV	Herne Bay, England	606.3
1946	Edward Donaldson	Gloster Meteor IV	Littlehampton, England	615.8
1947	Al Boyd	Lockheed P-80-R	Muroc, California	623.7
1947	Turner Caldwell	Douglas D-558-I	Muroc, California	640.7
1947	Marion Carl	Douglas D-558-I	Muroc, California	650.8
1947	Richard Johnson	North American F-86A	Muroc, California	671.0
1952	J. Slade Nash	North American F-86D	Salton Sea, California	698.5
1953	William Barns	North American F-86D	Salton Sea, California	715.7
1953	Neville Duke	Hawker Hunter	Littlehampton, England	727.6
1953	Mike Lithgow	Supermarine Swift	Azizia, Libya	735.7
1953	James Verdin	Douglas XF4D-1	Salton Sea, California	752.9
1953	Frank Everest	North American YF-100A	Salton Sea, California	755.1
1955	Harold Hanes	North American F-100C	Edwards Air Force Base, California	822.3
1956	Peter Twiss	Fairey Delta II	Chichester, England	1,132.1
1957	Adrian Drew	McDonnell F-101A	Edwards Air Force Base, California	1,207.6
1958	Walter Irwin	Lockheed F-104A	Edwards Air Force Base, California	1,404.1
1959	Georgi Mossolov	E-66	Podmoskovnoe, USSR	1,483.9
1959	Joseph Rogers	Convair F-106A	Edwards Air Force Base, California	1,526.0
1961	R. B. Robinson	McDonnell F4H	Edwards Air Force Base, California	1,606.3
1961	Hunt Hardisty	McDonnell F4H	Edwards Air Force Base, California	902.2[2]
1962	Georgi Mossolov	E-166	Podmoskovnoe, USSR	1,665.9
1965	Robert Stephens	Lockheed YF-12A	Edwards Air Force Base, California	2,070.1
1969	Darryl Greenamyer	Grumman F8F-2	Edwards Air Force Base, California	482.5[3]
1976	Eldon Joersz	Lockheed SR-71A	Edwards Air Force Base, California	2,193.6
1977	Darryl Greenamyer	Lockheed F-104	Tonopah, Nevada	997.0[2]
1979	Steve Hinton	Red Baron RB-51	Tonopah, Nevada	499.1[3]

[1]landplane record when ASR held by a seaplane [2]low-altitude record when ASR held at high altitude [3]piston-engine record when ASR held by a jet

Superwheels & Thrill Sports

Airplanes
AEROBATICS
AIRPLANE RACING
FLYING-MODEL AIRPLANES
HELICOPTERS
HOME-BUILT AIRPLANES
PERSONAL AIRPLANES
RECORD-BREAKING AIRPLANES
SCALE-MODEL AIRPLANES
YESTERDAY'S AIRPLANES
UNUSUAL AIRPLANES

Automobiles & Auto Racing
AMERICAN RACE CAR DRIVERS
THE DAYTONA 500
DRAG RACING
ICE RACING
THE INDIANAPOLIS 500
INTERNATIONAL RACE CAR DRIVERS
LAND SPEED RECORD BREAKERS
RACING YESTERDAY'S CARS
RALLYING
ROAD RACING
TRACK RACING

CLASSIC SPORTS CARS
CUSTOM CARS
DINOSAUR CARS: LATE GREAT CARS
    FROM 1945 TO 1966

FABULOUS CARS OF THE 1920s & 1930s
KIT CARS: CARS YOU CAN BUILD YOURSELF
MODEL CARS
RESTORING YESTERDAY'S CARS
VANS: THE PERSONALITY VEHICLES
YESTERDAY'S CARS

Bicycles
BICYCLE MOTOCROSS RACING
BICYCLE ROAD RACING
BICYCLE TRACK RACING
BICYCLES ON PARADE

Motorcycles
GRAND NATIONAL CHAMPIONSHIP RACES
MOPEDS: THE GO-EVERYWHERE BIKES
MOTOCROSS MOTORCYCLE RACING
MOTORCYCLE RACING
MOTORCYCLES ON THE MOVE
THE WORLD'S BIGGEST MOTORCYCLE RACE:
    THE DAYTONA 200

Other Specialties
BALLOONING
KARTING
MOUNTAIN CLIMBING
RIVER THRILL SPORTS
SAILBOAT RACING
SOARING
SPORT DIVING
SKYDIVING
SNOWMOBILE RACING
YESTERDAY'S FIRE ENGINES
YESTERDAY'S TRAINS
YESTERDAY'S TRUCKS

Lerner Publications Company
241 First Avenue North, Minneapolis, Minnesota 55401